Sing the Name

Sing the Name

The Meaning and Significance of Thirty-Six Devotional Chants

As Sung in

SIDDHA YOGA MEDITATION ASHRAMS AND CENTERS

PUBLISHED BY SYDA FOUNDATION
A SIDDHA YOGA MEDITATION PUBLICATION

As you chant
your heart becomes golden
and light radiates from your soul.

SWAMI CHIDVILASANANDA

Published by SYDA Foundation
371 Brickman Rd., P.O. Box 600, South Fallsburg, New York
12779, USA

Acknowledgments

This book is the offering of a great number of dedicated people. The project was initiated and the manuscript prepared by Kyra and John Myers with the support of Leonard Saphier. Information about the chants and their melodies was offered by Viju Kulkarni and Meg Christian. Dr. Hans Georg Turstig gave guidance on the Sanskrit, Valerie Sensabaugh was the copyeditor, and Peggy Bendet served as the coordinating editor. Cheryl Crawford was the designer and typesetter, and Osnat Shurer and Sushila Traverse oversaw production.

Printed in the United States of America

97 98 99 00 01 02 03 04 05   5 4 3 2 1

Library of Congress Cataloging-in-Publication Data

Sing the name : the meaning and significance of thirty-six devotional chants as sung in Siddha Yoga meditation ashrams and centers.
p. cm.
English and Sanskrit (romanized)
ISBN 0-911307-61-3 (pbk. : alk. paper)
1. Hinduism—Prayer-books and devotions—English. 2. Hinduism—Prayer-books and devotions—Sanskrit. I. SYDA Foundation.
BL1236.22.S56 1997
294.5'433—dc21 97-41994
CIP

The poem by Lalleshwari is from *Lalleshwari*, rendered by Swami Muktananda (South Fallsburg, N.Y.: SYDA Foundation, 1981).

The verse from the *Sāma Veda* is from *The Holy Vedas*, trans. by Pandit Satyakam Vidyalankar (Delhi: Clarion Books).

The verses from *Jñāneśvarī* are from *Jnaneshwar's Gita*, rendered by Swami Kripananda (Albany, N.Y.: State University of New York Press, 1989).

CONTENTS

FOREWORD

Chanting can fill us with joy and love, purify our surroundings, free us from anxiety, lead us into meditation, clothe us in contentment, secure our liberation, bring us face to face with God. As a musician, I have been tempted to ascribe much of this potential of chanting to the power of music, especially to that of singing. Singing is a universal human activity, one that seems to be programmed into our collective nature. Most people either love to sing, or wish they could. In more than twenty years as a voice teacher, I have never met anyone who didn't have some deep desire to be able to sing, and this has been most true of those who thought they couldn't sing at all! But everyone can sing. It's a natural part of our humanity.

Physically, singing is satisfying in ways that nothing else can quite duplicate. Breathing deeply, generating the sound within one's own body, feeling the musical vibrations enliven and inhabit the body, blending one's own voice with those of others or with instruments, hearing the resultant harmonies even as one continues to sing — these are enormously satisfying sensory experiences. Singing also has its psychological rewards: it is fun, it produces a general sense of well-being, and it can be very inspiring. When one sings great music, the sensory satisfaction and the musical inspiration can intersect in moments of startling beauty, offering rare and powerful glimpses of the divine. Anyone who has sung or heard fine performances of Bach's *Mass in B Minor* or the Brahms *Requiem*, for example, has undoubtedly known moments of intense revelation. Such peak experiences have something in common with what happens to us when we chant, namely, the state of ecstasy. But peak experiences are rare and fleeting, and subject to all manner of conditions. Is everyone in tune? Is the tone quality appropriate? Is the tempo too fast or too slow? And so on. In chanting, ecstasy is not achieved only in moments of fleeting glory. It is, rather, a steady, repeatable state, characterized as much by contentment as by elation.

The music of the chants is at least partly responsible for this phenomenon. The chant melodies of Siddha Yoga are rooted in the classical Indian system of ragas, in which a series of notes — as few as five and as many as twelve — are grouped together in characteristic patterns intended to evoke specific spiritual qualities or states of being. The word *rāga* means "that which colors the heart." Thus a particular chant may promote feelings of peace, joy, courage, or devotion. Chant melodies are very compact, usually consisting of only one or two phrase groups which are repeated over and over again. This repetition breaks the normal linear structure and dramatic narrative that characterizes most of the music we know in the West and replaces it with a more circular or spiral form, one in which each repetition takes us deeper into the very essence of the chant. It is almost as if the chant begins to sing us, rather than the other way around. In this way, the chant becomes part of our identity, and we are filled with the prevailing mood of the raga.

Repetition also serves as the perfect vehicle for absorbing and understanding the chant texts. In Western vocal music the plane on which text and music meet is a sublime and treacherous ground. It is sublime because when text and music fully complement each other, even the most inexpressible ideas and emotions find a voice. This process is what the famed choral conductor Robert

Shaw described as "the Flesh becomes Word," and it represents one of the highest forms of artistic expression. But a perfect relationship between text and music is not always easily or successfully accomplished; failure occurs just as often as success. Even the most beautiful or profound text can be trivialized if it is poorly set or it is set to inappropriate music. In chanting there is a different dynamic at work in the relationship between music and text. The chant texts used in Siddha Yoga are mantras, i.e., sacred words or divine sounds that have the power to protect, purify, and transform the individual who repeats them. Often these mantras are simply different forms of the divine name. The relationship between these mantras and the melodies that carry them is not about artistic expression. It is about the power of sound, and the power of mantras expressed as sound. The music prepares us by evoking in us the appropriate devotional attitude, and of course it carries the sound of the mantras to us. But it is the mantras themselves that are both means and ends. Certainly this has been my experience with chanting.

When I first heard about Siddha Yoga meditation, what I was really interested in was meditation, not chanting. Then, on my first visit to a center, I heard a tape of *Oṃ Namaḥ Śivāya*. Although I liked the music, I was most drawn to the sound of the mantra. It had a hauntingly familiar quality, as if I had heard it before. And then as it was repeated, I never had the feeling that I'd heard enough of it. This self-generating quality — that as soon as it ended, it began again — was effortless, as if it were repeating itself endlessly. I had the feeling that this sound, the mantra, was the missing piece of the puzzle in my life. There was an *aahhhh* feeling, as if to say, "At last, I'm home."

In the weeks and months that followed this first exposure, chanting brought the mantra into the very center of my existence: I could feel its vibration; I could hear it singing within me. Eventually, I could even see it animating the world, so that after a time, the words of the Kashmiri saint Lalleshwari, who lived some six centuries ago, became true for me:

> O Lalli!
> With right knowledge,
> open your ears and hear
> how the trees sway to *Oṃ Namaḥ Śivāya*,
> how the wind says *Oṃ Namaḥ Śivāya* as it blows,
> how the water flows with the sound *Namaḥ Śivāya*.
> The entire universe
> is singing the name of Shiva.

By now my life had been transformed. Obstacles suddenly were less daunting, the hard edges of daily life softened, and I was truly content for the first time that I could ever remember. As I look back, it is clear: it was the power of chanting that changed my life; it was the power of chanting that led me to pursue Siddha Yoga meditation; it is the power of chanting that keeps me on the path, even today.

Knowing the meaning of the chants dramatically increases our experience of their power. The Siddha Master Swami Muktananda used to say that when one chants with true understanding, it increases the power of the chant a thousand times. Such is the promise of *Sing the Name*: to provide us with detailed knowledge of the beloved chants, the *nāmasaṃkīrtanas* that have been chosen by the Siddha Yoga Gurus, that have been designated by them for spiritual practice. In this way, we can chant with true understanding. In the following pages we find not only transliterations of each chant, but word-for-word translations, often with several meanings for each word or name. As we read through the chant texts, we learn, for example, that God in the form of Lord Krishna is variously identified as "dark blue-black" or the "dark one," as the embodiment of God's love or the protector of the Lord's devotees. Further, Krishna's boyhood names Govinda and Gopala refer to him as "gatherer of cows," "protector of cows," and "master of the senses," and, as Narayana, Krishna becomes "the path for human beings to reach the divine," as well as "the goal itself." Such a rich tapestry of meanings and associations enlivens our experience, drawing us step by step ever deeper into the profound mystery of the divine name.

The translations are also accompanied by relevant background information that helps us imbibe the qualities of a particular chant. For example, about *Śrī-Rām Jay Rām* we learn that the melody of this chant "evokes the qualities of valor and courage on the spiritual path."

Chanting is a powerful and mysterious practice. No amount of explanation can reveal all its secrets. We learn about chanting by chanting. In *Sing the Name* the divine name is elucidated for us in all the glory of its subtle variations. In these pages we learn of different ragas and the feelings associated with the chants. We also find the words of the saints — Baba Muktananda, Gurumayi Chidvilasananda, Jnaneshwar, and many others, Siddhas all — whose vision of chanting inspires us. So, let us take their words to heart and chant. Chant with understanding and devotion, and revel in the power and grace that chanting brings.

John H. Guthmiller
June 1997

John H. Guthmiller is the director of choral activities and an associate professor of music at Virginia Commonwealth University in Richmond, Virginia, and the director of music at Richmond's Second Presbyterian Church.

A Note on the TRANSLITERATION

The names of God celebrated here are in the Sanskrit language. There are also songs honoring the spiritual Master Swami Muktananda, his Guru Bhagawan Nityananda, and other saints, and these are often in Hindi. Throughout the book, the standard transliteration scheme for South Asian languages has been used with the following exceptions: proper names, place names, and those terms most frequently found in Siddha Yoga books. These appear in the text in roman type with simple transliteration. *Śaktipāta*, for instance, appears as shaktipat; and the *kṛṣṇa* of the chants appears as Krishna in the explanatory text.

For those readers not familiar with Sanskrit and Hindi, the following is a guide to pronunciation.

Vowels

Vowels are categorized as either long or short. In English transliteration, long vowels are indicated with a macron, a horizontal line over the vowel, with the exception of the *e* and the *ai*, and the *o* and the *au*, which are always long.

Short:	Long:	
a as in c*u*p	*ā* as in c*a*lm	*o* as in kn*ow*
i as in g*i*ve	*ī* as in s*ee*n	*ai* as in *ai*sle
u as in f*u*ll	*ū* as in sch*oo*l	*au* as in c*ow*
ṛ as in wr*i*tten	*e* as in *e*ra	

Consonants

The distinguishing features of consonants in these languages is in the aspirated and retroflexive letters.

The aspirated letters have a definite *h* sound. The letter *dh*, for instance, is pronounced as in lan*dh*older; the letter *bh* as in clu*bh*ouse.

The retroflexes are pronounced with the tip of the tongue touching the hard palate; *ṭ*, for instance, is pronounced as in an*t*; *ḍ* as in en*d*.

The sibilants, which are often confused, are *ś*, *ṣ*, and *s*. The *ś* is pronounced as *sh* but with the tongue touching the soft palate; the *ṣ* as *sh* with the tongue touching the hard palate; the *s* as in hi*s*tory.

Other distinctive features are these:

c as in *ch*urch	*ñ* as in ca*ny*on
ch as in pit*ch*-*h*ook	*ṃ* or *ṅ* as a strong nasal
ph as in loo*ph*ole	*ḥ* as a strong aspiration

AN INVITATION TO CHANT

from a talk given at Shree Muktananda Ashram

Good morning. I am delighted to be with you this morning for soon we will be chanting together, and I love to chant. I know you do, too. When we chant together, we join a holy community, a sacred *saṅgha*, that extends far beyond these walls. Devotees all around the world relish the practice of chanting. And the Guru's sacred community extends even beyond this, into the distant past as well. The spirits of untold numbers who have celebrated their love for God throughout many centuries also join us when we open our hearts to chanting.

Our practice of chanting is known as *nāmasaṃkīrtana*, a term that comes from classical India. The Sanskrit word *saṃkīrtana* means "putting together" or "composing," and it also means "proclaiming" and "celebrating." The word *nāma* means "name." Here it refers to the name of God, and so it connotes the attributes of God. Thus when we sing *nāmasaṃkīrtana*, we compose ourselves, celebrate the divine name on our lips, and draw forth divine qualities from our hearts.

For as we come to experience through the Guru's precious gift of inner awakening, of shaktipat, godly qualities *do* reside within the heart — qualities like compassion, steadfastness, and humility.

These qualities yearn to burst forth from us, to swell outward into the world, like a gentle but irrepressible wind, bringing joy and celebration and transformation to all beings everywhere.

The practice of *nāmasaṃkīrtana* began in India many centuries ago. It was a gift of the saints. A saint sees divine qualities in every person he or she meets. A saint sees God in every person's eyes and hears God's word in every person's voice. The love that a saint has for all people flows from him, and so people are drawn to a saint, wherever he may be — in a public square or under a tree, in a temple courtyard or inside its inner sanctum. According to tradition, the saint would call out the glorious names of God, and the people who had gathered round would call those names back.

The saint and the seekers would sing together, and in their reverential echoing of God's attributes, the devotees would call forth from their hearts their own divine attributes.

It was a time for scholars to put aside their books and soldiers to lay down their arms, for businessmen to close their shops and laborers to retire from their tasks. Men and women from all walks of life would sit with the saint and open their hearts, singing the name of God.

Singing together, they formed the holy *saṅgha*.

Singing together, they brought forth their own love, their own innate joy, their own enthusiastic splendor.

The very syllables that they sang evoked in the singers deeply held virtues: tenderness, gratitude, reverence, affection, devotion, compassion, strength, and so many more.

Their words soared from their hearts and carried their love out to the world in all directions, even to the loftiest heights. A song from the ancient *Ṛg Veda* describes the words of a chant as "bright birds that fly to the heavens."

When we sing together, we join this ancient and ever-expanding community of the lovers of God. This is the holy community that Baba Muktananda brought with him when he introduced the majesty of Siddha Yoga meditation to the West. Baba taught us to chant. He taught us the wondrous and expansive practice of *nāma-saṃkīrtana*, inviting us to join that sacred *saṅgha*. Gurumayi Chidvilasananda has extended that grace-filled invitation to many more thousands of us.

And to accept that invitation, all we need do is free those "bright birds" and then let them soar. All we need to do is sing the divine Name in celebration of the divinity that is within us all.

William K. Mahony
August 3, 1997

William K. Mahony, professor of religion at Davidson College in Davidson, North Carolina, is the author of *The Artful Universe: An Introduction to the Vedic Religious Imagination*, published by State University of New York Press, and a co-author of *Meditation Revolution: A History and Theology of Siddha Yoga* from Agama Press.

Bolo Hare Rāma

bolo hare rāma hare rāma
rāma rāma hare hare
bolo hare kṛṣṇa hare kṛṣṇa
kṛṣṇa kṛṣṇa hare hare

Chant to Lord Rama, to Hari.
Chant to Lord Krishna, to Hari.

This chant has been sung by saints, sages, and devotees since ancient times. In it we chant the glory of two beloved forms of the Lord, Rama and Krishna. Both are divine incarnations of Lord Vishnu, who represents the sustaining principle of the universe. The word *bolo* means "chant," and *hare* means, "O Hari"; Hari is the "one who takes away": the remover of sorrow. Hari is also the "one who captivates" our hearts. Rama is the hero of the celebrated Indian epic the *Rāmāyaṇa*. *Rāma* means "delightful" or "pleasing."

Lord Krishna, here called the remover of all ignorance, imparts the sacred wisdom of the Divine to his disciple Arjuna in one of India's most venerated texts, the *Bhagavad Gītā*. The word *kṛṣṇa* means "dark blue," a color sometimes seen in deep meditation. As we chant these names of God, we invoke the joy and wisdom of our own highest consciousness.

The words of this chant are traditional, known throughout India.

Devakī-nandana Gopāla

devakī-nandana gopāla
gopāla gopāla devakī-nandana gopāla
devakī-nandana gopāla
devakī-nandana gopāla

Divine cowherd,
darling son of Devaki [Lord Krishna].

As a boy in Vrindavan Lord Krishna tended the cows, and one of his names is Gopala, "protector of the cows." *Gopāla* also implies one who is protector of the earth. *Devakī-nandana* is a term of endearment for Krishna, meaning "son of Devaki." Krishna is one of the most beloved forms of the Divine and is worshiped throughout India. He was so enchanting and irresistible as a boy that he is addressed here as the endearing child.

This was a favorite chant of Gadage Maharaj, a contemporary of Baba Muktananda, who set up facilities to feed and house the poor. The melody is based upon the *bilāval rāga*, which evokes the peaceful repose of the late morning.

Govinda Jaya Jaya

govinda jaya jaya gopāla jaya jaya
rādhā-ramaṇa-hari govinda jaya jaya

Salutations again and again to Govinda.
Salutations to Gopala.
Salutations to the beloved of Radha.
Salutations to Hari.

The power of the Divine that sustains the universe is known in India as Vishnu. According to the Vedic tradition, from time to time throughout the ages, he has manifested on Earth in human form. One of the most beloved of these forms was Lord Krishna. As a youth, when he was a cowherd, Krishna was known as Govinda and Gopala. The names refer to "one who gathers and protects the cows." The image of the cow is richly symbolic, referring to the Lord's protection of those who take refuge in him. The word *go*, which means "cow," also means "rays of light" and symbolizes the divine effulgence within each human being.

Rādhā-ramaṇa is a name for Krishna that means "the beloved of Radha." Radha was one of the *gopīs*, the milkmaids of Vrindavan, who were all supremely devoted to Krishna. Radha represents *śakti*, the divine energy, and so *rādhā-ramaṇa* also signifies one who delights in supreme Shakti, that energy in the form of the Goddess. *Hari* is "one who captivates" our hearts, "one who removes" our ignorance, and *jaya* means "hail," or "victory to."

In this chant we sing, “Hail to the Lord, victory to the Lord who protects us, who gives us refuge, who captivates us with his love.” Chanting his name, we can experience that he exists within us as our own delight, as our own divine inner Self.

The words of this chant are traditional. It is in the *bilāval rāga*, invoking the peaceful repose of the late morning.

Hare Rāma Hare Kṛṣṇa

hare rāma hare rāma
rāma rāma hare hare
hare kṛṣṇa hare kṛṣṇa
kṛṣṇa kṛṣṇa hare hare

Lord Rama, O Hari, Lord Krishna, O Hari.

Saints, sages, and devotees have sung this chant since ancient times, and in our present age, Kali Yuga (the Age of Iron), it has a special significance. In these times, almost every aspect of righteous order is disrupted; when we sing this chant, we invoke divine protection for ourselves and for others. Baba Muktananda loved this chant, and he often held what he called *saptahs* in which the names of Rama and Krishna were sung all day and all night for as long as a week. (This is where the term *saptah* came from; it means "seven.")

Hare means "O Hari." Hari is the "one who steals," thus, the one who takes away our ignorance, our sorrow and suffering. Hari is also the one who captivates us; he steals our hearts. *Rāma* means one we "delight" in, the "beautiful, pleasing" one. *Kṛṣṇa* means "the dark one" or "dark blue" — the color of Consciousness, seen in deep states of meditation. Lord Krishna embodies God's divine love and protection. In this ancient chant, we sing to Rama and Krishna, two beloved forms of the Lord who represent our own highest consciousness.

This chant is a powerful sixteen-syllable mantra. One version is based upon the *bhairavī rāga*, a melody of devotion, sung in a slow tempo and evoking a deep yearning for union with God.

Chanting is a significant and mysterious practice. It is the highest nectar, a tonic that fully nourishes our inner being. If we want to experience love, the greatest means is chanting God's name. Chanting opens the heart and makes love flow within us. It releases such intoxicating inner bliss that simply through the nectar it generates, we can enter the abode of the Self. Gauranga, Mirabai, Namdev, and many other great saints attained perfection by chanting the Name.

SWAMI MUKTANANDA

Hari Hari Bol

Refrain

hari hari bol hari hari bol
mukunda mādhava keśava bol

mukunda mādhava keśava bol
narahari viṭṭhaḷa nārāyaṇa bol

nityānanda muktānanda paramānanda bol
oṃ guru jaya guru jaya jaya guru bol

pāṇḍuraṅga śrīraṅga ātmaraṅga bol
nīlakaṇṭha meghaśyāma hari hara bol

jñānadeva tukārām nāmadeva bol
zipruaṇṇa sāīnātha nityānanda bol

kānhopātrā muktābāī janābāī bol
mīrābāī jagadambe sakhūbāī bol

mīnākṣī annapūrṇā kāmākṣī bol
cāmuṇḍī mahādevī kuṇḍalinī bol

Refrain

hari hari bol hari hari bol
mukunda mādhava keśava bol

Sing the names of Lord Krishna: the remover of ignorance, the bestower of liberation, the sweet one who gives the nectar of the Self, the one who conquered the demon Keshi.

This chant is a joyous exaltation of the names of God and of the saints. Each verse rings out in celebration of an aspect of the Lord or the name of a great saint. In this chant, we praise the great beings whose grace illumines the path to God. *Hari bol!* exclaims its melodious refrain. "Sing [the name of] Hari," the one who removes our suffering and captivates our hearts.

mukunda mādhava keśava bol
narahari viṭṭhaḷa nārāyaṇa bol

Mukunda, Madhava, and Keshava are names of Krishna, an incarnation of Lord Vishnu, the sustaining power of God. *Mukunda* means "granter of liberation." *Mādhava* is "the sweet one," the one who gives the nectar of the Self. *Keśava* is "the one who conquered the demon named Keshi."

Narahari refers to Vishnu in his incarnation as the man-lion Narasimha, who saved a child from the wrath of his demonic father. In this way, it could be said that *narahari* means "one who takes away our human limitations." *Viṭṭhaḷa* is the "one who stands on a brick," a reference to the Lord of Pandharpur, a form of Krishna worshiped by the poet-saints of Maharashtra for centuries. (See *Jay Jay Viṭṭhaḷa*, page 20.) *Nārāyaṇa* is a name of Lord Vishnu, the refuge of all creatures; it means "the path by which a human being reaches God."

nityānanda muktānanda paramānanda bol
oṃ guru jaya guru jaya jaya guru bol

In this verse we sing to the great Siddha Gurus, Bhagawan Nityananda and Swami Muktananda. The word *nityānanda* means "everlasting bliss," or "the bliss of the eternal." *Muktānanda* means "the bliss of one who is liberated, the bliss of one who is free." *Paramānanda* is "the highest bliss," the unchanging state of a liberated being.

Oṃ is the sacred, primordial vibration, the origin of all creation. The word *guru* is composed of the syllables *gu*, symbolizing "darkness," and *ru*, symbolizing "light"; the Guru is the one who leads us from the darkness of ignorance to the light of Self-realization. *Guru* also means "great" or "weighty," here in the sense of venerable and important. *Jaya* means "hail!" or "victory to!" So this verse says, "Hail to the Guru, the liberating and grace-bestowing power of God."

10 pāṇḍuraṅga śrīraṅga ātmaraṅga bol
nīlakaṇṭha meghaśyāma hari hara bol

Pāṇḍuraṅga refers to Lord Vitthala and means "one with white limbs," indicating purity and the presence of grace. *Śrī* denotes brilliance and splendor, beauty and auspiciousness, and *raṅga* means "color" or "quality." This is a name of Lord Vishnu, the "one of auspicious qualities" and also the witness of all our actions. *Ātmaraṅga* means "the color of the Self," one whose "color," or quality, is Consciousness.

Nīlakaṇṭha is the "blue-throated one," referring to Shiva, whose throat was stained blue when he consumed the poison that might have destroyed humankind. *Meghaśyāma* is a name of Krishna, meaning one who is "dark blue as a cloud." The image of dark clouds is a reference to the life-giving rain clouds of the Indian monsoon. Rain, in this case, is likened to knowledge of the Self, because this knowledge gives one true life. *Hari* is the one who removes suffering, and *hara* means "destroyer," the aspect of Lord Shiva that destroys ignorance.

jñānadeva tukārām nāmadeva bol
zipruaṇṇa sāīnātha nityānanda bol

This verse honors some of the poet-saints and Siddhas of Maharashtra, who were greatly loved by Baba Muktananda. This region of western India has been home to a great number of saints and is now the location of Gurudev Siddha Peeth, the mother ashram of Siddha Yoga meditation. *Jñānadeva* is an affectionate name for Jnaneshwar Maharaj, a Siddha who, at age fifteen, composed one of the great spiritual works of the world, *Jñāneśvarī*, a beautiful, poetic commentary on the *Bhagavad Gītā*. Tukaram was a householder-saint who wrote thousands of *abhaṅgas*, ecstatic songs to the Lord in the Marathi language. Namdev, a simple tailor, was also a great Siddha, known for his love of the name of God.

Zipruanna was the mysterious sadhu who sent Baba to Bhagawan Nityananda, the great Siddha who became his Guru. *Sāīnātha* is Sai Baba of Shirdi, a contemporary village saint who turned thousands of hearts to God.

kānhopātrā muktābāī janābāī bol
mīrābāī jagadambe sakhūbāī bol

In this verse, Baba honors some of the great women saints of India. The first three lived in Maharashtra. Kanhopatra was the dancer who merged with Lord Vitthala while chanting in his temple in Pandharpur, Muktabai was a Guru at the age of ten, and Janabai worked in the household of her Guru, Namdev. Janabai used to sing Lord Krishna's name all through the night;

then during the day Krishna himself would come to help her with her work.

Mirabai was a queen of Rajasthan who renounced the life of the court to devote herself to singing the divine name of Krishna. Jagadambe is the supreme Goddess, the Mother of the universe. And Sakhubai was a great devotee of Lord Krishna. When her family prevented her from going to the temple with other devotees, Krishna disguised himself and took her place at home.

mīnākṣī annapūrṇā kāmākṣī bol
cāmuṇḍī mahādevī kuṇḍalinī bol

This verse honors the supreme Shakti, the creative power of the Lord, in many of her forms. Minakshi is the beautiful daughter of Kubera, the lord of wealth. Annapurna bestows an abundance of life-giving food. Kamakshi is the "lovely-eyed" one.

Chamundi is another name for Durga, who is the slayer of the demons named Chanda and Munda. Mahadevi is the "great Goddess" or the "great Shakti." Kundalini is the divine Goddess within who, having been awakened by the Guru, brings us to God-realization.

The refrain is a traditional Indian chant; the verses were composed by Baba Muktananda in 1975, while on tour in Oakland, California. Baba's name was added to the second verse after his *mahāsamādhi*. The melody of this chant is based on *bhairavī rāga*, a late morning raga that evokes a devotional mood of tenderness and longing.

He Bhagavān

he bhagavān he bhagavān
jaya guru muktānanda tuma ho mahān
śaraṇa aye ham tumhāre
rakṣā karo bhagavān

O divine Lord! O divine Lord!
Salutations to the Guru, Muktananda.
You are the great one.
We have taken refuge in you.
O Lord, please protect us.

He Bhagavān resonates with reverence and love for the Guru, who safeguards the seeker on the spiritual path. The chant invokes the protection of *bhagavān*, the one who has attained what the Indian scriptures call the six great glories: absolute might, righteousness, glory, beauty, knowledge, and nonattachment.

He means "O," as in O Lord. *Bhagavān* is the "beloved one," or divine Lord, the possessor of great spiritual wealth and power.

Jaya means "victory to" or "hail." *Guru* is the "spiritual Master" or the "true teacher," and *muktānanda* means "the bliss of freedom." Thus the beginning of the chant says, "Hail to the Guru, to Muktananda, the one who is ever absorbed in the bliss of freedom." *Tuma ho mahān* means "you are great."

Śaraṇa aye ham tumhāre means "we have taken refuge in you." *Rakṣā karo bhagavān* asks, "O Lord, please protect us." In this chant, the protection we are seeking is to be safeguarded from our negative tendencies such as anger and fear, greed and envy — the obstacles that might prevent us from attaining the goal of the spiritual path, the state of inner perfection and supreme bliss.

The melody of this chant is based upon *bhīmpalāsī* or *bhīmpalāśrī*, a serious raga associated with the early afternoon and evoking peace and tenderness.

He Govinda He Gopāla

he govinda he gopāla
nārāyaṇa nārāyaṇa
nārāyaṇa rakho śaraṇa

O gatherer of the herd, protector of the earth [Lord Krishna], Lord Narayana, you are the path that leads us to the Divine. Protect us and give us refuge.

In this chant we sing to Lord Krishna and Lord Narayana, two incarnations of Lord Vishnu, the power of God that sustains all creation. As was said earlier, Govinda and Gopala are names for the young Krishna as a cowherd. *Govinda* means "the one who gathers the cows," and *gopāla* means "the one who protects the cows" or "protects the earth"; here these names also refer to the Lord as the gatherer and protector of his devotees. *He* is used to call out to the Lord and means "O," O Lord.

Nārāyaṇa means "the path for human beings to reach the Divine" — *nāra* is "human" and *ayana* is "the path." Lord Narayana is also the goal itself. *Rakho śaraṇa* means "protect us and give us refuge."

In this chant we sing, "Protect us, O Lord, impart your grace and wisdom to us, and show us the path to God-realization."

This chant was adapted from a traditional Indian *bhajan*, or devotional song. It is based on *deś*, a night-time raga, a sweet, plaintive melody that evokes aspiration and longing for God.

Listen to the melodious music of the divine poet.
He plays upon the flute of love —
the notes soar to heaven
and reach the distant stars
and dance on the raging waves of the sea.
The earth, the sea, the sky, the stars
are all woven together
by the soft strains of the divine music.
Its vibrations echo through the corridors of time
in the endless canopy of the sky.

SĀMA VEDA

Jay Jay Muktānanda

jay jay muktānanda
muktānanda jay jay
gaṇeśpurī nivāsī
jagadguru muktānanda

*Salutations again and again to Muktananda.
Salutations to the one who dwells in
Ganeshpuri, to the universal Guru.*

This chant expresses love and gratitude to Baba Muktananda. Chanting his name can invoke in us the state of divine freedom that this great Siddha possessed.

Jay is "hail" or "salutations," and *muktānanda* means "the bliss of one who is free"; we sing, "Salutations again and again to Baba Muktananda."

Gaṇeśpurī nivāsī refers to "one who dwells in Ganeshpuri," the village where Baba lived with his own Guru, Bhagawan Nityananda, and where he later founded Gurudev Siddha Peeth, the mother ashram of Siddha Yoga meditation.

Jagad means "universe," and *guru* means "Master" or "true teacher." Since Baba's grace, his subtle power, reaches all parts of the world, he is addressed as *jagadguru*, "the universal Guru."

"Hail to Muktananda, the one who dwells in Ganeshpuri yet exists everywhere, and who is also within us as our inner feeling of bliss."

The melody, which was composed by the musician Hari Om Sharan, is based on *pilū rāga*. This is a light raga that can be played at any time of day but is usually associated with the early evening.

Jay Jay Rām

jay jay rām kṛṣṇa hari
rājarām kṛṣṇa hari

Salutations again and again to Lord Rama.
Salutations to Lord Krishna.
Salutations to Hari.

Rāma and Krishna are incarnations of Lord Vishnu, the aspect of God that sustains and upholds creation. *Jay* means "hail" or "salutations." *Rām* or *Rāma* means "delightful, pleasing." Lord Rama was the perfect embodiment of dharma, of duty and right action. In the great Indian epic *Rāmāyaṇa*, Rama rescues the world from the malevolent Ravana. This story has a deeper meaning: just as Rama defeats this powerful demon, God's grace rescues us from our ignorance, our negativities, and our attachment to the senses.

Rājarām refers to Lord Rama or King Rama. (*Rāja* means "Lord" or "King.") *Kṛṣṇa* means "the dark one," referring to Krishna's dark blue color, the color of absolute Consciousness seen in deep meditation. He embodies divine love, the pure and blissful love of God that is ever present as the true nature of all things. *Hari* means both "the one who captivates" and "the one who takes away." Thus the Lord is the one who captivates our hearts and takes away our suffering and limitations.

The words of this chant are traditional, as is the melody, which is not based on a recognized raga. A version has been chanted in *bhairavī rāga*, a late morning raga that evokes the ache of separation from God and the longing for union with him.

Jay Jay Viṭṭhaḷa

jay jay viṭṭhaḷa jaya hari viṭṭhaḷa
jay jay viṭṭhaḷa jaya hari viṭṭhaḷa

Salutations to Lord Vitthala.
Salutations to Lord Hari.

The sustaining power of God is personified in Lord Vishnu, and one of his forms is Lord Vitthala. For centuries, people from all over India have made an annual pilgrimage to have the darshan of Vitthala's statue in the village of Pandharpur, joyfully chanting Vitthala's name along the way.

Viṭṭhaḷa means "one who is standing on a brick." It is said that Lord Vitthala stood on a brick to wait while Pundalika, his great devotee, dutifully finished attending to his (Pundalika's) ailing parents.

Hari means "one who takes away" our limitations. *Jay* and *jaya* both mean "salutations" or "hail." *Jaya hari viṭṭhaḷa* says, "Hail to the luminous Lord, the one who removes our limitations and reveals the truth." This chant celebrates the subtle presence of Lord Vitthala, who exists as the inner Self of all.

This is a traditional chant based on the *kāliṅgdā rāga*, a melody evoking feelings of quiet, awe-inspiring adoration, and the tenderness that characterizes the early morning hours. Another version, often used at dancing *saptahs*, is based on *bhairavī rāga*, a raga that is usually associated with the late morning and that evokes an intense longing for union with God.

Jay Jay Viṭṭhaḷa Pāṇḍuraṅga Viṭṭhaḷa

jay jay viṭṭhaḷa pāṇḍuraṅga viṭṭhaḷa
puṇḍalīka-varada pāṇḍuraṅga viṭṭhaḷa

Salutations again and again to Lord Vitthala,
the luminous one of bright color.
Salutations to the one who blesses
his great devotee, Pundalika.

Lord Vitthala is an incarnation of Vishnu, the sustaining power of the Lord. Vitthala had many devotees, but the greatest was Pundalika. So great was Pundalika's devotion that Lord Vitthala stood on a brick to wait while Pundalika finished caring for his elderly parents. (One meaning of *viṭṭhaḷa* is "one who is standing on a brick.") In the village of Pandharpur there is a statue of Lord Vitthala in a temple where he is portrayed standing on the brick offered by Pundalika.

Jay means "hail." *Pāṇḍuraṅga* means the "one of white limbs," referring to his great purity and the presence of grace. *Puṇḍalīka-varada* means "the one who answers the prayers of Pundalika."

The traditional words of this chant are set to the classical Indian *yaman-kalyān rāga*, whose melody has been described as peaceful, joyful, and invoking great blessings. The time for this raga has not been established, but it is often played in the early evening.

Let the sound of the chant strike you
like lightning. Let it flow through your body.
Then you will be in the chant.
You will love chanting. Gratitude will arise
spontaneously, and you will swim
in the ocean of nectar.

SWAMI CHIDVILASANANDA

Jaya Jaya Śiva Śambho

jaya jaya śiva śambho
jaya jaya śiva śambho
mahādeva śambho
mahādeva śambho

Salutations again and again
to Lord Shiva, to Shambho.
Salutations to Mahadeva.
Salutations to Shambho.

The grace-bestowing qualities of Lord Shiva are praised in this chant. Shiva is the primordial Guru and the source of absolute knowledge; he destroys all obstacles on the spiritual path, granting the bliss of God-realization.

Jaya means "salutations," or "hail." *Śiva* is the auspicious one, who is the indwelling Self of all beings. *Śambho* names the one who brings happiness and supreme joy, the abode of bliss. *Mahādeva* describes the "supreme Lord, great God" who exists everywhere and who shines in the hearts of all beings.

Jaya jaya śiva śambho says, "Hail to the supreme Lord, the auspicious one, the bringer of happiness and joy, who dwells as the Self in the hearts of all."

The melody of this chant is based on the classical *darbārī rāga*. This majestic raga suggests valor and grandeur and is associated with the time after midnight.

Kāli Durge

kāli durge namo namaḥ
kāli durge namo namaḥ
kāli durge namo namaḥ

Again and again, I honor
the goddesses Kali and Durga.

Kali and Durga are warriors who destroy the limitations that prevent us from recognizing that God dwells within us. These great goddesses are manifestations of the divine *śakti*, God's power of creation.

Kāli means "O black one"; she is the mother of time. Through her grace one is able to transcend the limitations of time and find peace in the eternal and limitless Self. Kali is the fierce aspect of the goddess, the one who destroys ignorance and grants Self-realization. *Durge* means "O Durga"; Durga is the one who is "difficult to conquer." *Namo namaḥ* means "I offer my salutations again and again."

Chanting the names of these fiery but benevolent goddesses, we invoke our own inner *śakti*, which conquers our ignorance and reveals the glorious splendor of the inner Self.

The melody of this chant is based on the *mānd rāga*, which has its origin in the traditional folk music of Rajasthan. It evokes a light and joyful mood and can be played at any time.

Kṛṣṇa Govinda

kṛṣṇa govinda govinda gopāla
kṛṣṇa govinda govinda gopāla
kṛṣṇa muralī manohara nandalāla

Lord Krishna, Govinda, Gopala.
Lord Krishna, heart stealer, flute player,
the son of Nanda.

In this joyous chant we sing some of the many names of Lord Krishna. *Kṛṣṇa* means "the dark one," referring to his dark blue color, the hue seen in deep meditation, the color of divine Consciousness. *Govinda* refers to Lord Krishna as the "gatherer of the cows." It also means the master of the senses, for Govinda helps us control the outgoing senses and turn our attention within. *Gopāla* is the "protector of the cows," a reference to Krishna's youth among the herdsmen of his beloved village, Vrindavan. Chanting this name recalls his playful and endearing qualities, as well as his nature as the divine protector.

Muralī manohara is the "one who steals our hearts while playing his flute." Krishna's music was so enchanting that when the *gopīs*, the milkmaids who were his greatest devotees, heard the sweet notes of Krishna's flute, they would stop everything and run to be with him. The great love story of all time, *raslīla*, is an account of the delightful play that unfolded when Krishna sounded his flute and hundreds of *gopīs* left their homes to spend loving hours with him — each thinking that she alone was with God. *Nandalāla* describes Krishna as "the son of Nanda."

In this melodic chant, we invoke God as the one who gathers in and protects his devotees, and whose divine love steals their hearts. Chanting the names of Krishna, we experience that his great qualities exist and resonate within our own deepest Self.

This lilting version of *Kṛṣṇa Govinda* is in the popular *bhairavī rāga*, a late morning raga that evokes a devotional mood of tenderness, peace, and longing.

Chanting the name of God is a yoga.
It has great śakti. *That* śakti *stills the mind*
and fills the heart with love.
Chanting destroys worry and pain
and creates joy. It purifies the atmosphere
both within and without. It kills the germs
of restlessness in the mind. Whoever
chants God's name with enthusiasm
is filled with divine bliss.

SWAMI MUKTANANDA

Mere Bābā Muktānanda

mere bābā muktānanda
mere bābā muktānanda
oṃ muktānanda oṃ muktānanda
oṃ muktānanda mere bābā muktānanda

My Baba Muktananda.
Oṃ, *Muktananda.*
My Baba Muktananda.

In this chant we express our love and devotion for the great Siddha Master, Baba Muktananda. When we sing this chant, a feeling of contentment is awakened, as well as the knowledge that the Guru is ours and we are his.

Mere means "my" and *bābā* is a term of endearment and respect. *Muktānanda* means "the bliss of one who is free, the bliss of one who is liberated." This is the state in which Baba lived, the state he has made available to seekers. *Mere bābā muktānanda* expresses our love and gratitude to this great teacher.

Oṃ is the primordial sound vibration of the universe, the source of everything. *Oṃ muktānanda* says, "Muktananda, you have the bliss of one who is free; you are the embodiment of the primordial sound of the Absolute." Chanting Baba's name with focus and love, we unite ourselves with the state of spiritual freedom and bliss that is inherent in the inner Self.

The melody of this chant is based on *darbārī-kānaḍā*, reflecting a royal, stately nature.

Muktānanda Mahān

muktānanda mahān jaya sadguru bhagavān
jaya sadguru bhagavān

Salutations to the true Guru, to the Lord,
to the great Muktananda.
Salutations to the true Guru,
to the Lord who possesses all greatness.

In this chant, which precedes the recitation of the *Guru Gītā* text every morning, we honor Baba Muktananda as the *sadguru*, the true Guru, and we salute his supreme state of spiritual freedom. This joyful state is the birthright of everyone, the nature of the inner Self. *Muktānanda* means "the bliss of one who is liberated," and *mahān* means "great." *Jaya* is "hail, salutations, victory to." *Sadguru* refers to the "perfect Master" who imparts the experience of the truth. *Bhagavān* describes the "illustrious Lord," the one who possesses the six great glories: absolute might, righteousness, glory, beauty, knowledge, and detachment.

Thus the meaning of this chant is "Hail to the great one, who comes in the form of the spiritual Master, who leads us to the bliss of inner freedom. Salutations to Baba Muktananda!"

This stately and dignified melody is based on the magnificent *darbārī rāga*.

Namaḥ Śivāy

namaḥ śivāy oṃ namaḥ śivāy
pārvatī-vallabha namaḥ śivāy
pārvatī-vallabha namaḥ śivāy
pārvatī-vallabha namaḥ śivāy

Salutations to Shiva.
Salutations again and again to Shiva,
the beloved of Parvati.

Lord Shiva is the supremely auspicious one, and the divine Shakti is the goddess Parvati. It is said that Lord Shiva lives on Mount Kailasa, which represents the *sahasrāra*, the highest spiritual center in the crown of the head. Shiva remains on Kailasa for thousands of years at a time, engrossed in meditation, transcendent, free from all support. However, in that state he is also inaccessible, and therefore, the Indian scriptures say, it is through Shakti, Parvati, that he can be known. Just as heat is inseparable from fire, Shiva is inseparable from Parvati; she is his means of acting in the world.

Namaḥ means "salutations," and *śivāya* means "to Shiva." So *namaḥ śivāy[a]* means "salutations to Shiva," the auspicious one, the indwelling Lord of all. *Oṃ* is the primordial sound of the universe. Parvati is the daughter of the holy mountain, and here Shiva is called *vallabha*, "beloved of Parvati" or "dearest." In this devotional chant to Shiva and Parvati, we invoke the love and bliss that exist within each of us as our inner Self.

This chant is based upon the *bilāval rāga*, which evokes the peaceful repose of the late morning.

Nārāyaṇa

nārāyaṇa nārāyaṇa jaya govinda hare
nārāyaṇa nārāyaṇa jaya gopāla hare

Salutations to Narayana,
to Govinda, to Hari.
Salutations to Narayana,
to Gopala, to Hari.

The protecting and nourishing power of the Divine is celebrated in this chant. Narayana is a name of Lord Vishnu, the aspect of God that sustains and supports everything in the universe. *Nāra* means "human" and *ayana* means "path." Thus, *nārāyaṇa* is "the path by which human beings reach God-realization." Lord Narayana is also the goal of liberation itself. *Jaya* means "hail" or "victory." *Govinda* and *gopāla* are two names of Lord Krishna from his youth as a cowherd; they refer to the Lord as the supporter and protector of the earth. *Hare* means "O Hari"; Hari is the "one who takes away" our ignorance and impurities.

In this chant, the words of which are traditional, we invoke the protection of the Lord, who sustains the world and who provides refuge for his devotees. He removes all obstacles that prevent us from knowing the divine nature of our own inner Self. By chanting these names of Lord Krishna, we experience the Lord's power and protection arising within ourselves.

Sing the songs of celestial love,
O singer! May the divine fountain
of eternal grace and joy
enter your soul.
May the Lord stay there forever!
May you always feel the presence
of the Lord within
as it plucks the strings of your soul
with the celestial touch.

Bless us with a divine voice
and may we tune
the harp strings of our life
to sing songs of love to You.

ṚG VEDA

Nityānanda Mahān

nityānanda mahān jaya sadguru bhagavān
jaya sadguru bhagavān

Salutations to the true Guru,
to the Lord, to the great Nityananda.
Salutations to the true Guru,
to the Lord who possesses all greatness.

Bhagawan Nityananda is honored in this chant as the *sadguru*, the true spiritual Master. We salute the greatness of this extraordinary Siddha, Baba Muktananda's Guru, who was continuously immersed in the state of divine bliss. Bhagawan Nityananda entrusted Baba with the mission of uplifting humanity by empowering people to realize that state within themselves.

Nityānanda means "eternal bliss," and *mahān* means "great." *Jaya* is "hail, salutations, victory to." *Sadguru* refers to the highest Guru, the "true spiritual Master." *Bhagavān* is the Lord, "the beloved one," the one who possesses the six divine qualities: absolute might, righteousness, glory, beauty, knowledge, and detachment.

Thus, this chant says, "Hail to the great one, the true Guru, who leads us to the state of eternal bliss. Salutations to Nityananda!"

This melody is based on the stately *darbārī rāga*, traditionally sung late at night.

Nityānandaṃ Brahmānandaṃ

nityānandaṃ brahmānandaṃ
brahma-svarūpaṃ nīlavarṇam
triloka-nāthaṃ śrī-gurudevam
oṃ namo nityānandaṃ

I honor Bhagawan Nityananda,
the bliss of the Absolute,
the manifestation of Brahman, the blue being,
the Lord of the three worlds, the divine Guru.
Oṃ, *I honor the supreme Nityananda.*

Bhagawan Nityananda, Baba Muktananda's Guru, was loved and revered throughout India as a supreme saint. He lived in the highest state of spiritual bliss and freedom, and he had the power to grant that state to others.

The term *nityānandaṃ* means "eternal bliss," and *brahmānandaṃ* means the "bliss of Brahman," the Absolute. *Brahma-svarūpaṃ* is the "very embodiment of Brahman," the supreme Lord, and *nīlavarṇam* refers to the "blue being." Blue is the color of supreme Consciousness, which can be seen in deep meditation.

Triloka-nāthaṃ means "Lord of the three worlds." (The three worlds are usually thought of as heaven, hell, and the mortal world, but this can also be understood as the three states of consciousness: waking, dreaming, and deep sleep.) *Śrī* is a term of respect, and *gurudevam* means "divine Guru." *Oṃ* is the primordial sound of the universe, the source of all creation. *Namo* means "I honor."

"Salutations to Bhagawan Nityananda, who lives eternally in a state of absolute bliss, who is the divine Guru of all the three worlds."

This chant was created in the village of Ganeshpuri in honor of its beloved saint, Bhagawan Nityananda. It is based on the *kalyān* or *yaman rāga*, a soothing melody that is said to invoke great blessings. It is associated with the early evening.

Oṃ Bhagavān

oṃ bhagavān oṃ bhagavān
oṃ bhagavān muktānanda bhagavān
oṃ bhagavān oṃ bhagavān
oṃ bhagavān muktānanda bhagavān

Oṃ, *Bhagawan.*
Oṃ, *Muktananda Bhagawan.*

Oṃ Bhagavān is a chant of extraordinary power, which honors the Lord in the form of the Guru. *Oṃ* is the sound-form of the Absolute. It is the primordial vibration, the sound which contains all other sounds and from which all creation has sprung. *Bhagavān* refers to the Lord, the possessor of great splendor and glory, of excellence and fortune. *Muktānanda* means "the bliss of one who is liberated."

In this chant, we sing the glory of the Guru, who is one with the Absolute, who always experiences the ecstasy of freedom, who dwells in the splendor of the Self, and who imparts his grace to us so that we can also experience that divine splendor. Chanting *Oṃ Bhagavān* evokes awe at the majesty of the supreme Lord and tender feelings of devotion and gratitude to the Guru.

The melody of this exquisite chant is based on the majestic melody *darbārī-kānaḍā*, which is said to evoke the deep stillness and the peace of midnight.

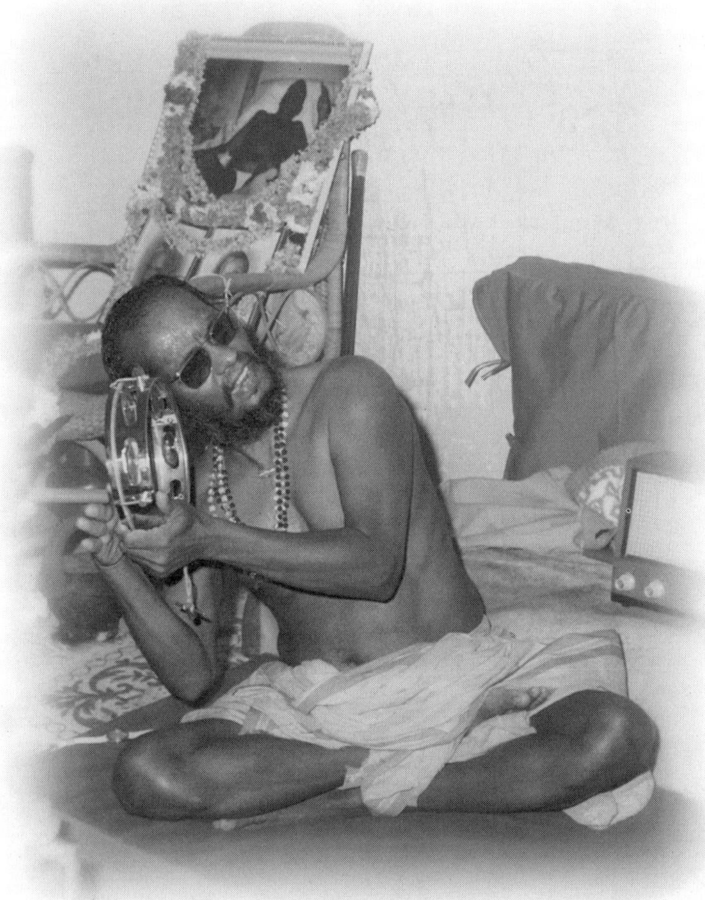

In the Bhagavad Gītā,
Lord Krishna has praised devotion.
"O Arjuna, I am attained by one who sings
My name steadfastly and ceaselessly.
I am attained by him who offers
his salutations to Me all the time, saying
'O Bhagawan, O Bhagawan.'
One who worships Me in this way
buys me very cheaply."

SWAMI MUKTANANDA

Oṃ Guru Jaya Guru

oṃ guru jaya guru saccidānanda guru
saccidānanda guru muktānanda sadguru

Oṃ, *salutations to the Guru,*
whose essence is Existence,
Consciousness, and Bliss.
Salutations to Muktananda, the true Guru.

The scriptures and sages say this entire universe springs forth from the word of God. That primordial sound is *Oṃ*. By chanting this sacred syllable, which is the root of all chants and mantras, we can experience the source of creation resonating within. The word *guru* signifies one who is full of light, who is fully imbued with wisdom. The two syllables *gu* and *ru* signify "darkness" and "light" respectively. The Guru is one who takes us from the darkness of ignorance to the light of knowledge.

Jaya means "hail." *Saccidānanda* refers to the three attributes of the Divine: Existence, Consciousness, and Bliss. The first syllable, *sat*, means "absolute Being"; *cit* is "supreme Consciousness"; and *ānanda* means "highest Bliss." The Guru, who has merged with God, lives in the state of *saccidānanda* — beyond limitation, supremely free and blissful, with perfect awareness of the Self. When we chant, we too can experience this state.

Baba's name, Muktananda, describes his state — "the bliss of one who is free, one who is liberated." *Sadguru* is the "true Guru." In this chant, we hail the Guru, Baba Muktananda, the embodiment of supreme Consciousness, the one who leads us to the state of perfect freedom that is the nature of the inner Self.

This chant was created by Baba in honor of his Guru, Bhagawan Nityananda, during a tour in India in 1969. Baba Muktananda's name was placed in the chant after he took *mahāsamādhi* in 1982. The melody is based on the *kalyān* or *yaman rāga*, which has been described as auspicious and the bearer of blessings; it is associated with the early evening.

Oṃ Gurudev

oṃ guru oṃ guru oṃ gurudev
jaya guru jaya guru jaya gurudev (2X)

Oṃ, *salutations again and again to the divine Guru.*

The ancient scriptures of India tell us that the primordial sound from which this entire universe springs forth is *Oṃ* — all other sounds are contained within it. Chanting this sacred syllable, the root of all chants and mantras, we can experience the holy vibration of the supreme Self resonating within.

The word *guru* literally means "heavy," signifying one who is full of power and wisdom, one with *śakti* to awaken the spiritual power in others. Since the Guru has attained oneness with God and his mind is firmly rooted in the highest reality, he has the power to help others achieve the greatest goal of human life — Self-realization. The syllables *gu* and *ru* signify "darkness" and "light"; thus the Guru is the one who destroys the darkness of ignorance and brings us to the light of knowledge.

Deva means "divine"; *gurudeva*, "divine Guru," signifies that the Guru is filled with the wisdom and grace of God and awakens that wisdom and grace within us.

Here we hail the Guru, the grace-bestowing power of God, who exists within us, who dispels the darkness of ignorance and awakens the light of true knowledge.

The melody of this chant is based on the classical *darbārī rāga*, which evokes the deep stillness and peace of midnight. It inspires feelings of devotion and longing for God.

Oṃ Namaḥ Śivāya

oṃ namaḥ śivāya

Oṃ, *salutations to Shiva.*

Baba called *Oṃ Namaḥ Śivāya* the great redeeming mantra. It has the power to redeem, or liberate, the one who repeats it, because it is charged with the full power of God. As the initiation mantra of the Siddha Yoga lineage, it carries the power of all the Siddhas who have repeated it through the ages. It is *caitanya*, alive, because of their grace. When we repeat *Oṃ Namaḥ Śivāya*, we can merge our awareness with that of God and transcend our human limitations, thereby experiencing the source of divine Consciousness, the inner Self.

Oṃ is the primordial vibration from which the whole universe has arisen. *Namaḥ* means "salutations," and *śivāya* means "to Shiva," the Absolute. *Oṃ Namaḥ Śivāya* means "I honor Shiva, the all-pervasive Self."

This powerful mantra has the capacity to purify the body and mind. As we chant, our awareness turns within to the immense peace and joy of the inner Self.

Oṃ Namaḥ Śivāya is sung in seven different melodies, including *darbārī*, a classical raga that evokes the deep stillness of midnight; *bhīmpalāsī*, a tender raga associated with the early afternoon; and *śiva bhairav,* a morning raga of grandeur and devotion.

There is so much sweetness in chanting.
There is so much nectar in the name of God,
you won't have to go to any holy place.
As you repeat the name of God,
your entire body becomes a holy place.
Your mind itself becomes a holy place.

TUKARAM MAHARAJ

Oṃ Namo Bhagavate Muktānandāya

oṃ namo bhagavate muktānandāya

Oṃ, *salutations to Muktananda. Salutations to the great Lord.*

Baba Muktananda devoted his life to the spiritual upliftment of humanity. *Oṃ* is the sacred, primordial syllable, the sound from which the entire universe has arisen. When we repeat *Oṃ*, we can experience the original creative energy that resides in the heart of each person. *Namo* expresses reverence and means "salutations."

Bhagavate is a form of the word *bhagavān*; it means "the generous one," the one who gives great spiritual wealth and power. Bhagawan is the great Lord, beloved for his benevolence, compassion, and light. *Muktānandāya* means "to Muktananda," which means "the bliss of the liberated one."

In this chant we honor the Guru, Bhagawan, the great one, who lives in the ecstasy of spiritual freedom and who awakens that freedom in us.

This chant was created in the village of Ganeshpuri, India, to honor Baba Muktananda's Guru, Bhagawan Nityananda. It was changed to include Baba's name after his *mahāsamādhi*. The melody was first based on *jhinjhoti rāga*, which evokes a mood of joy and longing. More recent versions of the chant are based upon different ragas. One version is based on the *bhūpālī rāga*, a nighttime raga that is dignified and stately, inspiring feelings of deep contentment, harmony, and detachment. Another version is based on the *dhani rāga*, which is the morning equivalent of the evening *malkauns rāga*. It is associated with the abundance and vibrancy at the heart of life and has the power to evoke unwavering happiness and strength, great courage, and confidence. A version created when Gurumayi Chidvilasananda was visiting New Zealand in 1997 is based on the *bhīmpalāsī rāga*, which sets a quiet mood of peace and tenderness. Another form, known as the *bhakti rāga*, evoking a light and joyful mood, has often been chanted at Shree Muktananda Ashram in South Fallsburg, New York. Yet another, known as *jīvanpurī rāga*, was created in South Fallsburg at the 1997 Guru Purnima celebration. The *jīvanpurī* or *jaunpurī rāga* is luminous and tender, a melody of active supplication associated with the late morning.

Oṃ Śiva

oṃ śiva oṃ śiva parātparā śiva
oṃkāra śiva tava śaraṇam
namāmi śaṅkara bhavānī śaṅkara
umā maheśvara tava śaraṇam

Oṃ *Shiva, the transcendent Reality,*
the source of all creation; I take refuge in you.
I bow to you, Shankara,
and to your śakti, *Bhavani.*
I take refuge in you, the great Lord,
united with your śakti, *Uma.*

In this joyful chant, we honor Shiva and Shakti, the Goddess here called by the names Bhavani and Uma. Shiva and his *śakti* dwell in our hearts, where they bestow great bliss. *Oṃ* is the primordial sound from which arises all creation. *Śiva* is the "auspicious one," the indwelling Self of all beings, the highest goal of life and the ultimate Reality. *Parātparā* means "beyond the beyond, higher than the highest." *Parātparā śiva* is supreme Shiva, the transcendent one, the Absolute.

Oṃkāra is the manifestation of *Oṃ* arising from the Absolute, from Shiva. *Śiva tava śaraṇam* says, "I take refuge in you, Shiva," the one who is my protector and my sanctuary.

Namāmi means "I bow" and is an expression of devotion. Shankara and Bhavani are Shiva and Shakti. Shankara represents Shiva as the one who bestows prosperity and blessings. *Bhavānī* is the Goddess, the one who takes us across the ocean of *saṃsāra*; she leads us over the ocean of worldly existence to the shore of liberation.

Umā means "she who is ever young," another name for Shakti. She is the origin of all, the place from which emerges all light and splendor. *Maheśvara* means the "great Lord." *Umā maheśvara tava śaraṇam* says, "I take refuge in you, O great Lord, Shiva, who are united with Shakti." The chant points us to the light of supreme Consciousness deep in our own hearts.

The melodious, sweet quality of this chant is based on the *kalyān* or *yaman rāga*, which is a soothing melody that attracts blessings and evokes joy and contentment.

Raghupati Rāghava Rājarām

raghupati rāghava rājarām
patita pāvana sītārām
patita pāvana sītārām patita pāvana sītārām
śrī-rām jay rām jay jay rām (3X)

The Lord of the Raghu dynasty, Lord Rama,
the uplifter of souls, inseparable from Sita,
salutations to Shri Rama.
Again and again, salutations to Rama.

In the Indian tradition, Lord Rama is an incarnation of Vishnu, the sustaining power of God, who came to Earth to restore righteousness. In the Indian epic *Rāmāyaṇa*, Rama rescues his wife, Sita, from the clutches of the evil, ten-headed Ravana, who represents the ego out of control. Just as Rama defeats this demon, God's grace rescues us from our negativities and ignorance.

Rāma means "pleasing, delightful." He is also called *raghupati*, meaning "Lord of the Raghus," the clan from which he came. *Rāghava* similarly means "of the Raghus," while *rājarām* means "Lord Rama," or "King Rama."

Rama is *patita pāvana*, "the one who uplifts us." *Sītārām* means "Sita's Lord Rama." *Śrī* is a term of respect, and *jaya* means "hail" or "victory."

As we hail Lord Rama, we invoke the divine power that dwells within us, that saves us from ignorance and frees us to live in harmony with the truth.

This chant is based on *pilū rāga*, a light melody appropriate at any time, though usually played at the end of the day.

Rāma Kṛṣṇa Hari

rāma kṛṣṇa hari mukunda murāri
pāṇḍuraṅga pāṇḍuraṅga pāṇḍuraṅga hari

Rama, Krishna, Hari,
the bestower of liberation,
the destroyer of the ego, the radiant one.

Lord Vishnu, the sustaining power of God, has taken on different forms in different ages for the upliftment of the world. Rama and Krishna are two of these forms. As Rama, the Lord returns dharma to the Earth, while as Krishna, he inspires devotion. *Rāma* means "beautiful" or "pleasing," and *kṛṣṇa* means the "dark one." *Hari* is the "one who takes away" our suffering and limitations; he destroys the cycle of birth and death by granting God-realization.

Mukunda is the "one who gives liberation," and *murāri* destroys ignorance. The base of the word *murāri* is *mura*, the name of one of the demons Lord Krishna destroyed. Demons symbolize the ignorance inherent in our limited ego. *Pāṇḍuraṅga*, another name for Krishna, means the "one of white limbs."

In this chant, we sing to the Lord whose love is irresistible, who removes all obstacles that keep us from knowing God within ourselves, who rescues us from the prison of our ego and grants us the boon of liberation.

The words of this sublime chant were taken from a traditional *kīrtana*, or devotional song from the villages of India. The melody is based upon the dignified *bhūpālī rāga*, which inspires feelings of deep contentment, harmony, and detachment.

O my mind, chant God's name;
chant it day and night. Only then will you
find true repose. You will not find true peace
through anything else. This path is very
easy, but it brings the highest bliss.
O Manpuri, by singing God's name,
become completely desireless and
delight in the inner Self.

MANPURI

Rāma Rāghava

rāma rāghava rāma rāghava
rāma rāghava rakṣa mām
kṛṣṇa keśava kṛṣṇa keśava
kṛṣṇa keśava pāhi mām

Lord Rama, Lord of the Raghu dynasty
and protector of all life.
Lord Krishna, the giver of liberation
and the sustainer of all life.

Rāma and Krishna are two of the most beloved incarnations of Vishnu, the aspect of God that sustains the world. *Rāma* means "pleasing" or "delightful," and he is the perfect embodiment of dharma. In the epic *Rāmāyaṇa*, Rama rescues his wife from the clutches of the demon Ravana — just as God's grace rescues us from our limitations and releases us from the prison of our ego.

Rama is referred to here by various names. He is called *rāghava*, meaning "of the Raghus," his ancestral clan. *Rakṣa mām* means "protect me," asking the Lord for protection from obstacles, both inner and outer, on the spiritual path.

Kṛṣṇa means the "dark one," referring to his dark blue color, the color of Consciousness seen in deep meditation. In the *Bhagavad Gītā*, Krishna imparts the secret of yoga to his disciple Arjuna and brings him to the realization of God within. *Keśava* is "slayer of the demon named Keshi" and *pāhi mām* says, "Sustain me."

This chant invokes the divine power that dwells within, which sustains and protects us, and which grants the glory of Self-realization.

Sāmba Sadāśiva

Refrain

sāmba sadāśiva sāmba sadāśiva
sāmba sadāśiva hara śambho

he girijāvara he girijāvara
he girijāvara hara śambho

he karuṇākara he karuṇākara
he karuṇākara hara śambho

he mṛtyuñjaya saccitasukhamaya
he karuṇāmaya hara śambho

Eternally united with Shakti, the eternally auspicious one, the destroyer of ignorance and the bestower of bliss [Lord Shiva].

Lord of the mountain-born Goddess, the destroyer of ignorance, and the bestower of bliss.

Embodiment of compassion, the destroyer of ignorance, and the bestower of bliss.

Conqueror of death; all-pervasive one whose essence is Existence, Consciousness, and Bliss absolute; compassionate one; the destroyer of ignorance and the bestower of bliss.

This lovely chant praises Lord Shiva and invokes his compassion and grace. *Sāmba* describes Shiva as forever united with the universal Mother, divine Shakti. *Sadāśiva* refers to the one who is always auspicious: *sadā* means "eternally," and *śiva* "the auspicious one." *Hara* means the destroyer, the one who removes spiritual ignorance. *Śambhu* is the source of bliss, the bestower of happiness, and the abode of joy.

He means "O," as in O Lord. *Girijāvara* describes "the Lord of the mountain-born Goddess" [Parvati].

Karuṇākara describes Lord Shiva as the "giver of compassion."

Mṛtyuñjaya is the "conqueror of death," another name for Lord Shiva. *Saccitasukhamaya* means "the one whose nature is all-pervasive Existence, Consciousness, and Bliss." *Karuṇāmaya* hails the Lord as the "compassionate one."

The chant says, "O Lord Shiva, you are eternally united with Shakti, the goddess Parvati, and you destroy our ignorance and bestow bliss. You are the embodiment of compassion, the conqueror of death, all-pervasive Existence, Consciousness, and Bliss." It is based on *kāfī*, a light, popular raga that evokes happiness and playfulness. It is associated with the night.

Śivāya Namaḥ Oṃ

śivāya namaḥ oṃ śivāya namaḥ oṃ
śivāya namaḥ oṃ namaḥ śivāya
oṃ namaḥ śivāya oṃ namaḥ śivāya

Oṃ, *salutations to Shiva.*

Śivāya Namaḥ Oṃ is a version of *Oṃ Namaḥ Śivāya* (see also page 45), the initiation mantra of the Siddha Yoga lineage. This sacred mantra purifies and steadies the mind, and awakens *kuṇḍalinī śakti*, the spiritual energy that exists within all human beings. *Oṃ Namaḥ Śivāya* has this capacity because it carries the power of all the Siddhas who have repeated it through the ages; it is *caitanya*, alive, because of their grace.

Oṃ is the primordial vibration from which the universe has arisen. *Śivāya namaḥ* means "salutations to Shiva," the eternal Absolute, the inner Self of all. Shiva pervades all beings and all things, and encompasses all the varied qualities and contradictions of this world. By repeating this mantra, we can come to see everything with the eye of equality, understanding that beauty and ugliness, delusion and truth, the joy of divine union and the pain of worldly suffering all spring from the same divine source.

Chanting the mantra has the power to awaken one to the experience of the inner Self. The mantra also possesses the power to protect the one who repeats it.

The melody of this chant is based upon *kāfī rāga*, a light nighttime melody that evokes happiness.

The truth is that God fills us completely
within and without, and it does not matter
whether we see him or not.
What matters is that we keep singing
his name joyfully all the time.

SWAMI MUKTANANDA

Śrī-Gurudeva-Śaraṇam

śrī-gurudeva-śaraṇam (3X)
nityānandaṃ brahmānandaṃ
sakalānandaṃ paramānandaṃ
nityānandaṃ-caraṇaṃ śaraṇam
muktānandaṃ-caraṇaṃ śaraṇam

I take refuge in the Guru.
I take refuge in Nityananda, in Brahmananda,
in omnipresent bliss, in the highest bliss.
I take refuge at Nityananda's feet.
I take refuge at Muktananda's feet.

In this chant, we honor the Guru and pray that he grant us protection and guide us safely on the spiritual path. *Śrī* is a title of respect, *guru* is the "true spiritual Master," and *deva* means "divine" or "effulgent." *Śrī-gurudeva* describes the spiritual Master who has realized his own divinity and is filled with the radiant wisdom and grace of God.

Śaraṇam means "refuge" or "surrender"; *Śrī-gurudeva-śaraṇam* says, "I take refuge in the divine Guru."

Bhagawan Nityananda was an extraordinary Siddha, the Guru of Baba Muktananda. His name means "eternal bliss," describing the unchanging ecstasy of spiritual liberation. *Brahmānandaṃ* is the "bliss of the Absolute."

Sakalānandaṃ means "the bliss of everything," and *paramānandaṃ* is "the highest bliss." In these lines, we honor the Guru's sublime state and pray for the grace to realize that state within ourselves.

Caraṇaṃ means "the Guru's feet," which, according to the yogic scriptures, hold the awesome power of the Guru's spiritual attainment. *Nityānandaṃ-caraṇaṃ śaraṇam* means "I take refuge at Bhagawan Nityananda's feet," and *muktānandaṃ-caraṇaṃ śaraṇam* means "I take refuge at Baba Muktananda's feet."

When we take refuge in the supremely blissful Guru, he protects us and imparts to us his own state of inner freedom.

The melody of this chant is based upon *deś*, a sweet, nighttime raga that evokes aspiration and longing.

Śrī-Kṛṣṇa Caitanya

śrī-kṛṣṇa caitanya prabhu muktānanda
hare kṛṣṇa hare rām rādhe govinda (3X)

Shri Krishna, the Lord, whose essence is
Consciousness and freedom.
O Hari, Lord Krishna, Lord Rama,
Radha, Govinda.

Ś*rī* is a form of respect meaning the "auspicious" one. *Kṛṣṇa*, the "dark" one, is an incarnation of Vishnu, who comes to Earth again and again to restore righteousness and dharma. In the *Bhagavad Gītā*, it was Lord Krishna who imparted the secret of yoga and selfless service to his disciple Arjuna on the battlefield of Kurukshetra.

Caitanya means "Consciousness," and *prabhu* is "the Lord"; *caitanya prabhu* is the Lord whose essence is Consciousness. Divine Consciousness is fully manifest in the Guru, Baba Muktananda, whose name means "the bliss of one who is free."

Hare means "O Hari," and refers to the "one who takes away" our ignorance. The Lord removes all the obstacles that keep us from knowing the inner Self.

Rām, the "delightful" one, is another incarnation of Lord Vishnu. In the Indian epic *Rāmāyaṇa*, Rama rescues his wife, Sita, from the demon-king Ravana, just as the Lord rescues his devotees from their inner enemies and negativities.

Rādhe govinda means "O Radha, O Govinda." Radha was foremost among the *gopīs*, the milkmaids of Vrindavan who were completely devoted to Krishna, and who became one with him through their devotion. Radha is also Shakti, the power of the Lord. *Govinda* means "the gatherer of the cows," referring to Krishna's boyhood as a cowherd.

We chant to the Guru for the grace to overcome our ignorance and realize the divine wisdom that exists within.

This chant is based upon the *bilāval rāga*. It evokes the peaceful repose of the late morning.

Śrī-Kṛṣṇa Govinda

śrī-kṛṣṇa govinda hare murāre
he nātha nārāyaṇa vāsudeva (3X)

All-powerful Krishna, O Hari,
you are the bestower of wisdom, the one
who destroys ignorance, the slayer
of the demon Mura.
O Lord, you are the indwelling divinity
and the divine refuge of all.

In this chant we sing to the Divine in the form of Lord Krishna. *Śrī* means "all-powerful, magnificent." *Kṛṣṇa* means "dark blue-black" and refers to his dark blue color, the color of Consciousness seen in deep meditation.

The name *govinda* derives from Krishna's boyhood as a cowherd; it means the "one who gathers the cows." *Go* means both "cow" and the "senses" or the "phenomenal universe," so *govinda* refers to the mastery of the physical senses in order to perceive God within.

Hare means "O Hari," and refers to the "one who takes away." The Lord, Hari, frees us from our limitations and negativities. *Murāre* says "O Murari," referring to the Lord as the "enemy of the demon Mura." The Lord slays the demon of our ego.

He nātha means "O Lord." Lord Krishna was an incarnation of Lord Vishnu, the sustaining power of the Divine, and another of his names is Narayana. *Nāra* means "human" and *ayana* means "the path," so *nārāyaṇa* is the "path for human beings to reach the

Divine," as well as the goal itself. *Vāsudeva* means "the indwelling Lord" and also the god of wealth.

As we chant, we invoke the Lord who gathers in and protects his devotees, who slays the demons of ego and ignorance, who assumes many forms, and who dwells within us as our own inner Self.

This chant is based on the classical *kalyān* or *yaman rāga*, whose melody has been described as peaceful and joyful, invoking great blessings.

Rarely does anyone reach heaven, but these saints have turned the whole earth into heaven. They have purified everything with the power of their chanting My name. . . .

I do not dwell in heaven, nor am I seen in the orb of the sun. More than that, I transcend even the minds of yogis.

Yet, O Arjuna, though I am lost to others, I must be sought in those who unceasingly chant My name.

How content they are, singing of My qualities! They forget even time and place, and in the joy of their song they experience inner bliss.

They joyfully recite My names — Krishna, Vishnu, Hari, Govinda — and engage in many enlightened discussions on the Self.

LORD KRISHNA IN *JÑĀNEŚVARĪ*

Śrī-Rām Jay Rām

śrī-rām jay rām jay jay rām

Salutations to Lord Rama.

Śrī-rām jay rām means "Hail to Lord Rama, the great and auspicious one." This mantra has been chanted in India since ancient times, and it plays a part in the epic poem *Rāmāyaṇa*, Lord Rama's life story. Rama, who is the embodiment of dharma, rescues his wife, Sita, from the demon-king Ravana. Rama is assisted in this heroic undertaking by Hanuman, the great monkey hero. Hanuman's unparalleled strength is exceeded only by his perfect devotion and service to Rama. The *Rāmāyaṇa* relates that Hanuman had repeated the mantra *śrī-rām jay rām* for many years before he finally met Rama. As a result, Hanuman's mind is so clear that he immediately recognizes Rama as his Guru, as the supreme Lord, and as the pure Consciousness within his own heart.

Śrī means "illustrious" or "revered." *Rām* (or *Rāma*) means the "delightful" one, the embodiment of righteousness, and *jay* means "hail."

Chanting Rama's name invokes the qualities and blessings of the inner Self, the pure and transcendent space within us that is full of light and purity.

One version of this classic chant has been sung at mealtimes in Siddha Yoga ashrams since 1965. This melody is not associated with any particular raga. Another version of *śrī-rām jay rām* is set to the *malkauns rāga*, a melodic form that evokes the qualities of valor and courage on the spiritual path. This melody was created in 1994 in Gurudev Siddha Peeth in Ganeshpuri, India, the mother ashram of Siddha Yoga meditation, to celebrate *hanumān jayantī*, Hanuman's birthday.

Viṭṭhaḷa Viṭṭhaḷe Pāṇḍuraṅga Viṭṭhaḷe

viṭṭhaḷa viṭṭhaḷe pāṇḍuraṅga viṭṭhaḷe
pāṇḍuraṅga viṭṭhaḷe pāṇḍharīnātha viṭṭhaḷe

Vitthala, the luminous one, the radiant one.
Vitthala, the Lord of Pandharpur.

Lord Vitthala is a beloved form of Lord Vishnu, the power of God that upholds and sustains all creation. This chant is a favorite of pilgrims traveling to sacred Vishnu shrines in India. *Viṭṭhaḷa* is the "one who stands on a brick." It is said that Lord Vitthala happily stood on a brick to wait while his devotee Pundalika finished caring for his aged parents. A temple was later built on the spot, where a statue of Vitthala on the brick stands today.

Pāṇḍuraṅga hails the brilliance of the Lord; it means "one of white limbs." *Pāṇḍharīnātha* means the "Lord of Pandharpur," the village where the temple of Lord Vitthala is located.

This is a traditional chant whose melody is based on the classical *pahādi rāga*. This light and pleasant raga, which can be played at any time of the day or night, is reminiscent of the folk music of India.

EPILOGUE

The power of chanting cleanses your entire being. It brings about auspiciousness and soothes a sad heart. The power of chanting is very healing. During the chant sometimes you may experience great ecstasy. At other times you may feel you are just mouthing the words. Don't worry about the state of your mind. Whether you are completely immersed in devotion or just skimming along the surface of the sound, the power of chanting seeps through your entire being.

When it is cold and you have a shawl, you only experience warmth if you wrap the shawl around you. The power of chanting is not like that. Whether or not you wrap the chant around you, you still reap the fruit. It will be with you when you need it most. Whether you sit and listen to the chant or fully bathe in its nectar, the power of chanting does its work. It burns away impurities. It gives you the power to have uplifting thoughts. It fills your heart with benevolence.

— *Swami Chidvilasananda*

The SIDDHA YOGA TRADITION

These thirty-six chants, which are from the spiritual traditions of India, are sung in Siddha Yoga meditation centers and ashrams all over the world. Singing these chants is a spiritual practice recommended by the Siddha Yoga Master Swami Chidvilasananda, an enlightened teacher who initiates and guides seekers on the spiritual path. Heir to a lineage of Siddha Masters, Swami Chidvilasananda received the power to transmit and guide spiritual energy from her own teacher, Swami Muktananda, who was himself initiated by the revered saint Bhagawan Nityananda.

On the path of Siddha Yoga, the experience of enlightenment — the fulfillment and freedom of perfect contentment — comes through the interplay between the Master's grace and the seeker's effort. Eventually the seeker becomes aware of his or her own perfection and perceives the bond of love that unites each one of us with God. This is the promise and the blessing of the lineage of Siddha Yoga Masters.

CHANTING BOOKS

The Nectar of Chanting

As Swami Muktananda writes in the Introduction to this book, "*Svādhyāya*, or chanting and reciting sacred texts, embraces all aspects of yoga and grants all its rewards." This useful book contains the chants frequently sung in Siddha Yoga meditation centers and ashrams, including the *Guru Gītā*, the morning and evening *Āratī*, and hymns honoring Shiva, Vishnu, Kundalini, and Mahalakshmi.

Shree Guru Gita

This small chanting book easily fits in a pocket or purse and is convenient for traveling. It contains the text of the *Guru Gītā* as well as the chants that are sung before and after the *Guru Gītā* in the daily recitation in Siddha Yoga ashrams and centers.

Shri Rudram

Shri Rudram, a chant that is sung in Siddha Yoga ashrams, is dedicated to Lord Rudra, the one who brings happiness and removes pain. (This book does not include English translation.)

Arati

Āratī is an ancient form of worship. A flame, symbolizing the individual soul, is waved before the form or image of a holy being. In Siddha Yoga ashrams, morning and evening *āratī* is performed to the statue of Bhagawan Nityananda, and a prayer, called simply "Arati," is sung. This prayer, which was created by Swami Muktananda in his Guru's honor, is accompanied here by mantras from the Upanishads, which are sung after the morning *āratī*, and the hymn called the "Shiva Arati."(This book does not include English translation.)

VIDEO *and* AUDIO CASSETTE TAPES *and* COMPACT DISKS

Many of the *kīrtanas* described in this book are available on video and audio cassette tape and CD. In audio, for instance, *Oṃ Namaḥ Śivāya* is offered in six different versions (including the *bhūpālī rāga* and *darbārī rāga*); *Oṃ Namo Bhagavate Muktānandāya* is in three versions; and *Śrī-Rām Jay Rām* is available in two. There are also videos of such chants as *Jay Jay Viṭṭhaḷa*, *Kāli Durge Namo Namaḥ*, and *Śrī Kṛṣṇa Govinda*. There are many other chants on audio tape and CD as well, and new ones are often recorded.

You may learn more about the teachings and practices of Siddha Yoga meditation by contacting:

SYDA FOUNDATION
P.O. Box 600, 371 Brickman Rd.
South Fallsburg, NY 12779-0600, USA
Tel: (914) 434-2000

or

Gurudev Siddha Peeth
P.O. Ganeshpuri, PIN 401 206
District Thana, Maharashtra, India

For further information on books in print by Swami Muktananda and Swami Chidvilasananda, and editions in translation, please contact:

SIDDHA YOGA MEDITATION BOOKSTORE
P.O. Box 600, 371 Brickman Rd.
South Fallsburg, NY 12779-0600, USA
Tel: (914) 434-2000 ext. 1700

Call toll free from the United States and Canada:
888-422-3334

Fax toll free from the United States and Canada:
888-422-3339